FRIENDS OF JESUS

STORIES AND ACTIVITIES FOR CHILDREN, PARENTS, AND TEACHERS

Victoria Hummell, R.A.

Illustrations by Gunvor Edwards

Liguori
LIGUORI, MISSOURI

Imprimi Potest:
Richard Thibodeau, C.Ss.R.
Provincial, Denver Province
The Redemptorists

Published by Liguori Publications
Liguori, Missouri
www.liguori.org
www.catholicbooksonline.com

Library of Congress Control Number: 2003109461

First published in United Kingdom in 2002 by McCrimmon Publishing Co. LTD, 10-12 High Street, Great Wakering, Essex, SS3 0EQ.

Text © 2002, 2003 by Victoria Hummell, R.A.
Illustrations © 2002, 2003 by Gunvor Edwards

ISBN 0-7648-1101-0

All rights reserved. No part of this publication may be reproduced, stored in a retrieval system, or transmitted in any form or by any means—electronic, mechanical, photocopy, recording, or any other—except for brief quotations in printed reviews, without the prior permission of the publisher.

Scriptures quotations are taken from the *Good News Bible*, published by the American Bible Society, © 1966, 1971, 1976, 1992. Used with permission.

Acknowledgments

I would like to express my thanks to my friends Sister Mary O'Gorman, R.A., Rev. Ieuan Wyn Jones, and Sister Mavis Langmead, R.J.M., who have spent their lives in the service of education and who have been, or are, Diocesan Religious Advisers. They read the text and offered their invaluable support through their criticism, encouragement, and help.

Page layout design by Nick Snode

Printed in the United States of America
07 06 05 04 03   5 4 3 2 1
First U.S. edition

Contents

Introduction 4

Jesus' Family
    Mary 6
    Joseph 9
    Elizabeth and Zechariah 12
    John the Baptist 15

Stories of Some of the Apostles
    Peter 20
    Andrew 24
    James 26
    John 29
    Philip 32
    Matthew 34
    Thomas 36
    Judas Iscariot 39

Other Friends of Jesus
    Mary of Magdala 44
    Martha and Mary 47
    Lazarus 50

Some People Who Helped Spread the Good News
    Paul 54
    Luke 58
    Barnabas 60

Notes for Parents and Teachers 63

Introduction

Dear Children,

This is a book about some of the people whom we read about in the New Testament. Some met Jesus during his life, some heard about Jesus after he had returned to Heaven after his death and Resurrection. All of these men and women loved Jesus, and their lives were changed because of his love for them. These were ordinary people like us. They listened to Jesus and wanted to tell others about him.

As you read this book and think about the activities you do, I hope you remember that you have been chosen by Jesus as his friend and that this will give you the courage to be a good friend of Jesus too.

Victoria Hummell, ra

Jesus' Family

The Gospels tell us about Mary (Jesus' mother), Joseph (his foster father), Elizabeth (Mary's cousin), Elizabeth's husband (Zechariah), and their son John the Baptist. We do not know very much about the family of Jesus or the beginning of Jesus' life on earth. What we do learn is all told in the first part of the Gospels. Mary is mentioned again in the Gospels, but we hear no more of Joseph.

Mary (Jesus' Mother)

ONE DAY when Mary was a young woman an angel named Gabriel appeared to her and asked her to be the Mother of Jesus, God's son. Mary was utterly astonished. At first she was afraid, but Gabriel reassured her by telling her that there was nothing to be worried about. She agreed to do what God asked her because she loved and trusted God.

Mary, who lived in Nazareth in Galilee, was engaged to Joseph. When it was nearly time for Jesus to be born, Mary and Joseph had to go to Bethlehem. It was there in a stable that Jesus was born. Joseph took care of Mary and helped her to bring up Jesus.

Soon after his birth, Mary and Joseph took Jesus to the Temple to be presented to God. While they were there they met Simeon and Anna, who were holy people and quite old. They spent all their time in the Temple praying. Simeon took Jesus in his arms and said a prayer. He described Jesus as a "light" that would show Jewish and non-Jewish people the way to God. Anna too was very happy and praised God when she saw Jesus.

When the parents brought the child Jesus into the Temple... Simeon took the child in his arms and gave thanks to God...

Luke 2:27

Mary, Joseph, and Jesus went back to live in Nazareth; that is where Jesus grew up and learned to love God. He was a carpenter like Joseph.

Mary and Jesus were invited to a wedding in Cana. There were a lot of people at the wedding and the wine ran out. Mary persuaded Jesus to provide more wine. He did this by changing water into wine. That was the first time he had ever worked a miracle.

At the end of Jesus' life Mary was there with him at the foot of the Cross, when he was crucified. She was full of happiness when Jesus rose from the dead and she was there with the Apostles in Jerusalem when the Holy Spirit came upon them all on the day of Pentecost. ➢

What do you think?

1. Look at the picture on page 6. How do you think Mary felt when the angel Gabriel asked her to be Jesus' mother?
2. Which story about Mary do you like best? Why?
3. Say the Hail Mary slowly to yourself, write the part you like best, say why. Draw a picture or make a pattern with a color to show its meaning.
4. How do you think Jesus felt when Mary asked him to provide more wine at the wedding?

Friends of Jesus

Mary (Jesus' Mother)

Think further and investigate

1. Mary has been given many titles; find out some of them. What do they tell us about her?

2. Find a hymn book and choose a hymn about Mary. Read the words aloud. What is it trying to say? Is it a good hymn? Does it help you understand and love Mary better?

3. In the New Testament, look up the Acts of the Apostles 1:12–14 and 2:1–4. What does this tell you about Mary after the death and Resurrection of Jesus?

4. What symbols and colors are often associated with Mary? What do they mean to you?

5. Find out what feasts of Mary are celebrated on March 25, September 8, August 15, and December 8. Find out more about one of those feasts and look at the readings for Mass that are said on that day.

Read what the Bible says

Read Luke 1:26–38, 2:1–40, John 2:1–12, John 19:25–27, and Acts 1:12–14 in the order in which they are given here. These New Testament parts tell the story of Mary.

Joseph

JOSEPH lived in Nazareth and made his living as a carpenter. He was engaged to marry Mary when he heard that she was going to have a baby. Because of that Joseph decided not to marry her. Soon after, though, he had a dream, during which an angel told him that the baby Mary was expecting would be called Jesus and was God and he would help people to love God. Joseph married Mary and took care of her and Jesus.

Just before Jesus was to be born Joseph traveled with Mary to Bethlehem because the Roman conquerors had ordered everyone ➢

Friends of Jesus

Joseph

to return to the place of their ancestors, as they were making a list of everyone who should pay taxes.

When Mary and Joseph arrived at Bethlehem the only place they could find to stay was a stable where animals lived. Mary gave birth to Jesus, and Joseph looked after them both. Shepherds and some Wise Men came to see baby Jesus.

 **What do you think?**

Mary and Joseph could only find a stable to stay in.

1. Look at the picture on page 9. Say what Jesus and Joseph might be talking about. What might Jesus be feeling?
2. Imagine you are Joseph. How would you feel if you could not find a place to stay in Bethlehem? What would you do to make the stable more comfortable?
3. What kind of person do you think Joseph was? What would he and Mary have taught Jesus at home and in his work?
4. Joseph and Jesus would have prayed the Psalms together. Look up Psalm 121; this is one of the Psalms that people used to sing as they were walking to Jerusalem. It says that our help comes from God, not from mountains. Pick out the verse or sentence you like best, copy it out, say why you have chosen it, and add your own prayer.

After a short time in Egypt, where they went to escape Herod, who wanted to kill Jesus, the Holy Family returned to Nazareth where Jesus grew up. Joseph taught him how to be a handyman. When Jesus was twelve Joseph and Mary took him to Jerusalem to celebrate Passover there.

Joseph died before Jesus; this is why just before he died Jesus asked John to look after Mary for him.

Joseph

Think further and investigate

1. Find out what happened when Joseph, Mary, and Jesus went to Jerusalem for the Passover by looking up Luke 2:41–52. Imagine you are Joseph. What will you say to Mary? What will you say to Jesus?

2. Are there any statues or pictures of Joseph in your school, at home, or in church? Look at them and notice what symbols Joseph has with him. What are they and what do they tell you about him?

3. During the Church's year there are two feast days of Saint Joseph. When are they? What does each one celebrate?

4. Joseph is the patron saint of many different places and people. Name some and tell their story.

5. Perhaps using the Internet or a CD-ROM, look up a great artist or an art gallery and find a picture of Joseph or a Nativity scene. How is he portrayed? What is the artist trying to show us?

6. Find a prayer to Joseph, read it thoughtfully and then make up one of your own.

Read what the Bible says

Read Matthew 1 and 2 and Luke 2:22–52 in the order in which they are given here. These New Testament parts tell the story of Joseph.

Elizabeth and Zechariah

ELIZABETH AND ZECHARIAH were John the Baptist's parents; they were holy people who faithfully followed God's law. All their married lives they longed to have children. One day when Zechariah was in the Temple in Jerusalem, taking his turn to offer incense because he was a priest, an angel appeared to him and told him that his wife, Elizabeth, was going to have a baby. This news was a big surprise because, although Elizabeth and Zechariah

Elizabeth and Zechariah

had prayed for a child for a long time, they were both quite old. In fact, Zechariah was so surprised he could not speak.

When Mary, Elizabeth's cousin, heard Elizabeth was going to have a baby, she hurried off to visit her. Elizabeth was really happy to see Mary. Mary showed how pleased she was to see Elizabeth by saying a special prayer we call the Magnificat. Mary stayed with Elizabeth until her cousin's baby was born.

Elizabeth was filled with the Holy Spirit and said in a loud voice, "You are the most blessed of all women, and blessed is the child you will bear!..."

Luke 1: 41–42

Elizabeth was very happy to see her cousin Mary.

When it was time for the baby to be given a name everyone thought he would be called after his father, but Zechariah wrote down that he was to be called "John." ➢

What do you think?

1. Look at the picture on page 12. Why are Elizabeth and Zechariah looking so happy?
2. Make a congratulation's card for the baby for Elizabeth and Zechariah.
3. Imagine that you are Elizabeth. How would you have felt when Mary arrived at your house?
4. Imagine that you are Zechariah. How did it feel to hear such exciting news and be unable to speak?
5. Think quietly by yourself for a few moments about how you praise God when you are happy, as Zechariah did; then write a short Praise prayer in honor of God's goodness.

Friends of Jesus ───────────────────────

Elizabeth and Zechariah

After that, Zechariah got his voice back and the first thing he did was to praise God.

You can find out more about this baby called John when you read the story of John the Baptist.

Think further and investigate

1. Look up the Magnificat in Luke's Gospel in chapter 1:46–55. Write down the line you like best and say why.
2. Find out what name is given to the prayer of Zechariah.
3. Find out who says this prayer every morning and the Magnificat in the evening (clue: ask a priest).
4. Use a CD-ROM or the Internet to find out more about the story of the Temple in Jerusalem and what it looks like.

Read what the Bible says

Read Luke 1:5–25, 39–80.

John the Baptist

JOHN THE BAPTIST was the son of Elizabeth and Zechariah. When he grew up he went into the desert to pray. He dressed in camel's-hair clothes with a leather belt and ate locusts and wild honey. He preached to the people and told them to be sorry for their sins (to repent), because God's kingdom was coming soon. He advised people on how to live better lives. He told them to share what they had with the poor, not to cheat each other, and not to be greedy. Some people did not like what he had to say, but John was very courageous and continued preaching. Some people thought ➢

Friends of Jesus

John the Baptist

John the Baptist came to the desert of Judea and started preaching. "Turn away from your sins," he said, "because the Kingdom of Heaven is near!"

Matthew 3:1–2

he was Christ the Messiah, but he explained that he was not and that he was not even good enough to undo Christ's sandals.

John baptized the people who repented.

John baptized the people who repented in the river Jordan as a sign of their friendship with God. One day, when John was baptizing, Jesus joined the line of people waiting to be baptized. When it was his turn, John said to Jesus, "It is you who ought to be baptizing me." Jesus replied, "No, you baptize me." So John did. As Jesus was coming up out of the water, the Holy Spirit appeared

 **What do you think?**

1. Look at the picture of John the Baptist on page 15. What does the picture show?
2. What did John tell the people to do? What would you tell people to do today to become better people?
3. Say what Jesus and John talked about together when they met by the river Jordan.
4. God spoke very lovingly to Jesus after his baptism by John. Make up your own prayer to tell Jesus how much you love him.

John the Baptist

over him in the shape of a dove, and God's voice could be heard saying, "This is my Son whom I love, I am very pleased with him." It was John's job to prepare the way for Jesus. He encouraged his own disciples to leave him and join Jesus. John was a very humble man.

Think further and investigate

1. Notice that the story of John the Baptist is recorded in all four Gospels. What does that tell you?
2. Find out the story of how John died. Write a few sentences to tell about what each person connected with the story of John's death is like.
3. Find a few pictures of John, maybe on an art gallery Web site. What symbols do the pictures show and why?
4. Find out when the church celebrates the feast of John the Baptist. Look up the readings or prayers for that day. Why do you think they have been chosen?
5. What does John the Baptist have to teach us today?

Read what the Bible says

Read Matthew 3:1–17, Mark 1:4–11, Luke 3:1–22, and John 1:19–37 in the order in which they are given here. The death of John the Baptist is found in Matthew 14:3–13, Mark 6:14–29.

Stories of Some of the Apostles

The Apostles were ordinary men Jesus met as he
traveled around. What made them special was that
after praying to God his Father (Luke 6:12–16),
Jesus invited them to follow him;
they were glad to accept this invitation.

Luke uses the word "Apostle" (which means *sent*)
in his Gospel when he tells us about the twelve
special followers of Jesus. The Apostles were
with Jesus as he taught and healed people.
They heard his stories and learned from him.

There are many stories in the Gospels about some of the Apostles and almost nothing about others. There is a list of the Apostles in Luke 6:12–16, Mark 3:16–19, Matthew 10:2–4, and the Acts of the Apostles 1:13.

After Jesus returned to Heaven the Apostles traveled far and wide spreading the Gospel, that is, the Good News of Jesus. That is how the Church began.

There was another large group of women and men who followed Jesus and were with him as he traveled around teaching and healing people. They were also there when he died and rose again. These are usually called disciples. They helped spread the Gospel also.

Peter

PETER and his brother Andrew were fishermen who lived beside the Sea of Galilee, probably at Capernaum. One day as Jesus was walking by the Sea of Galilee, he saw Peter and Andrew fishing; he called to them to follow him. They left what they were doing and immediately followed Jesus. Peter was married. When his mother-in-law was ill, Jesus healed her. Peter was with Jesus when he taught people by telling them stories and when he healed the sick.

Peter

After the Apostles had been with Jesus for a while, Jesus asked them who they thought he was. It was Peter who answered first. "You are Christ the Son of God," replied Peter. Jesus was delighted that he had understood who he was. (Peter had originally been called Simon.) Jesus told him that his name was to be Peter now, which means "rock." Jesus made him leader of the Apostles.

Jesus walked towards them on the water.

Peter was very enthusiastic, but sometimes he lost his confidence. One night he was out fishing with the other Apostles. Jesus was in the hills alone praying. It got so windy that they could not row to the shore. Jesus saw they were in trouble and walked towards them on the water. When Peter saw Jesus he thought he would walk across the water to meet him. Jesus encouraged him, but Peter suddenly felt afraid and started to sink. Jesus took him by the hand and told him to have more faith.

"This is my own dear Son, with whom I am pleased   licten to him!"

Matthew 17:5

Just after this, Jesus went up a mountain to pray and took Peter, James, and John with him. It was a very special time because the Apostles saw Jesus changed (transfigured) and heard God's voice say, "This is my Son whom I love, I am very pleased with him, listen to him." It was such a wonderful moment that Peter wanted to stay there longer, but Jesus knew there was work to do.

At the Last Supper, Jesus chose to wash the disciples' feet to show them how they should serve each other. When Jesus got to Peter, he did not want to let Jesus do this, but Jesus told him that if he refused he would not belong to him. ➢

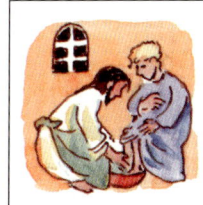

...he rose from the table, took off his outer garment, and tied a towel round his waist. Then he poured some water into a washbasin and began to wash the disciples' feet...

John 13:4–5

Friends of Jesus

Peter

"I am telling you the truth: before the rooster crows you will say three times that you do not know me."

John 13:38

So Peter said, "Well, then, will you wash my hands and head too?" Jesus explained that it was enough to wash his feet. Later on during the Last Supper, Jesus predicted that they would all leave him. Peter told Jesus that he would never leave him. Jesus told him that before the rooster had crowed three times he would deny that he even knew him. Peter was sure he would not. However Jesus was right; and when Jesus had been arrested, Peter denied that he knew him. When the rooster crowed, Peter remembered Jesus' words and was so very sorry that he cried. Later on, Jesus gave Peter the chance to make up for his denial of him.

After Jesus had risen from the dead, he told the Apostles to go back to Galilee. One day while they were out fishing they saw the risen Jesus on the shore. Peter recognized him first. Jesus made a fire and they all roasted fish on it. Afterwards Jesus asked Peter three times if he loved him. Peter replied each time that he did. This was his opportunity to make up for denying Jesus.

After the Holy Spirit came upon the Apostles on the day of Pentecost, Peter worked very hard to help spread the Good News about Jesus.

 **What do you think?**

1. Which story about Peter do you like best? Why do you like it? What does it tell you about Peter? Draw a picture of it.

2. Can you imagine how Peter felt when he first saw Jesus and Jesus asked him to follow him? Act out the story with a friend—one being Jesus and one being Peter. Talk to each other about what happened.

3. Jesus described Peter as a "rock" because he was solid and dependable. What name would you like Jesus to call you?

Peter

Think further and investigate

1. Why is Peter often shown holding keys? What does this mean? (Clue: look up Matthew 16:13–19.)

2. Find out why the most important church building in the Catholic Church is St. Peter's in Rome. The Internet may be able to help.

3. Find out when the two feasts of Saint Peter occur in the church calendar. What does each celebrate?

4. Look up and read the story about Peter and Tabitha in Acts 9:36–43. What does this story tell you about Peter? How has Peter changed during the time he followed Jesus?

5. Think of the qualities that Peter has and the ones you would like to have and make up a prayer about it.

You will find more stories about Peter when you read about the other Apostles.

Read what the Bible says

Read Matthew 4:18–22, Matthew 16:13–19, Matthew 8:14–16, Matthew 14:23–33, Matthew 17:1–9, John 13:6–11, Matthew 26:31–35, Matthew 26:69–75, John 21:15–17, and Acts 2:1–18 in the order in which they are given here.

Andrew

ANDREW was a fisherman. He had been a follower of John the Baptist. When John pointed out Jesus to him, Andrew went immediately to tell his brother Peter that Jesus was the Messiah: the one everyone had been waiting for. Later on when Andrew was fishing with his brother Peter, Jesus passed by and called them both to follow him and told them that he would make them fishers of people. They left their boats and nets and followed Jesus.

Andrew

People came in great numbers to listen to Jesus' words and to be healed. Jesus loved these people. One day when Jesus had been with them for a long time and it was getting late, he worried that they were getting hungry. Andrew brought a boy to Jesus who had five loaves of bread and two fish with him. Andrew told Jesus he thought it would not be enough to feed everyone. Jesus told him not to worry and took the loaves and fish and blessed them and told the Apostles to give them out. There was enough for everyone with plenty left over.

 **What do you think?**

1. Imagine how Andrew described Jesus to Peter when he first told him about Jesus. Tell about it.
2. With others, act out the story of the boy with his loaves and fish. Make up what you think each person might have said.

 **Think further and investigate**

1. Of which country is Andrew the patron saint?
2. Draw the flag of that country. How does the symbol on it connect with a story about Andrew?
3. Find out when Saint Andrew's day is. Look up in a Missal the prayer used on that day. What do you think about it? Make up a prayer of your own in honor of Saint Andrew.

 **Read what the Bible says**

John 1:35–41, Mark 1:16–17, and John 6:1–11 in the order in which they are given here.

James

JAMES and his brother John were fishermen who lived by the Sea of Galilee. They were mending their nets with their father Zebedee when Jesus invited them to join him. Like Andrew and Peter they immediately left everything and followed Jesus. Jesus nicknamed them *Boanerges,* which means *Sons of Thunder.*

Along with John and Peter, James was a very close friend of Jesus. Jesus chose James to be with him on special occasions. One day when Jesus was in Galilee, a man called Jairus, who was an official of the Jewish synagogue, came up to him and begged him to come

James

to his house because his twelve-year-old daughter was dying. But before they got to the house a man from Jairus' house arrived with the news that the young girl had died. Jesus told Jairus not to worry because, if he believed, his daughter would be restored to him. When they got to the house, Jesus took Peter, James, and John and the little girl's parents in with him. Jesus took the little girl's hand and helped her to get up. Her parents were amazed that she was alive again. Jesus told them to give her something to eat.

"...I have chosen you to be with me..."

Mark 3:14

After the Last Supper, Jesus went to the garden of Gethsemane to pray. He took his disciples with him, and left them to pray together. He then took Peter, James, and John further on so that they could be close to him while he prayed. They found it difficult to stay awake.

After the Apostles received the Holy Spirit on Pentecost day, James found he had the courage to spread the good news of Jesus.

What do you think?

1. Why do you think Jesus gave James and John the nickname Boanerges, meaning "Sons of Thunder"? What do think it means?

2. Do you have any special friends? Why are they special, and what do you share?

3. Imagine you are Jairus' daughter. Tell someone else what happened to you. What did you think when you saw Jesus?

Jesus took Peter, James, and John further on in the garden so that they could be close to each other while he prayed.

Friends of Jesus

James

Think further and investigate

1. Find out the date when the feast of Saint James is celebrated.

2. Sea shells are often used to symbolize James. Why would this be? What would you choose to symbolize yourself and why?

3. Find out which town in Spain is a special place of pilgrimage connected with James. Using a CD-ROM or the Internet, find out more about it.

Read what the Bible says

Read Matthew 4:21–22, Mark 3:17, Luke 8:40–42, 49–56, Mark 14:32–34, and Acts 12:1–3 in the order in which they are given here.

John

JOHN, like his brother James, was a fisherman. Jesus chose him to be his follower. He was often there at important times in Jesus' life. In the Gospel of John, John is sometimes called the "beloved disciple" because he was especially close to Jesus.

At the Last Supper, John was sitting next to Jesus, so when Jesus told the disciples that someone was going to give him up to his enemies, Peter asked John to find out who it might be. John asked Jesus who it was and Jesus gave them a clue. Later on that evening, Jesus took Peter, James, and John with him to the garden of ➤

Friends of Jesus

John

Gethsemane where he went to pray. After Jesus was arrested and taken to the High Priests' court, John was able to follow him in there and get Peter in, too, because he knew the high priest.

When Jesus was crucified, he thought of his Mother and he asked John to take care of her as he would his own mother. John took Mary home with him and looked after her. On the Sunday morning after Jesus was buried, Mary of Magdala came running back from Jesus' tomb saying that it was empty; Jesus was not there. Peter and John rushed off to find out what had happened. John got there first, but he waited for Peter to catch up. Peter went in first. They saw the cloths that Jesus had been wrapped in but he was not there.

Later Jesus appeared to the Apostles and helped them to understand that although he had died, he had risen from the dead as he promised he would.

John, like the other Apostles, began teaching people how Jesus had shown us God's great love and that in fact he loves us so much that he calls us his children.

What do you think?

1. Find a picture of John. What do you see in the picture and what does it tell you about him?
2. Why did Jesus ask John to look after his Mother? How do you show care for your Mother or Father?
3. Imagine what Peter and John said to each other when they found Jesus' tomb was empty.
4. Write or say a short prayer to thank God for his love.

John

Think further and investigate

1. What symbol is used to signify John's Gospel? Give a reason for the choice of symbol.

2. What clue did Jesus give his disciples about the identity of his betrayer? (John 13:23-26)

3. With whom did John speak to get into the High Priests' court? (John 18:15-17) Imagine you are John; how would you have felt about what went on in that court?

4. Why do you think that John waited for Peter to go into the tomb first? What does this tell you about the characters of John and Peter? What would you have thought if you had been John and found the tomb empty?

5. Read 1 John 3:1-2. What do those words mean to you? How might these words change the way you act?

Read what the Bible says

Read Mark 1:19-20, Mark 3:17, Mark 14:32-34, John 13:23-26, John 18:15-17, John 19:25-27, John 20:1-10, and 1 John 3:1-2 in the order in which they are given here.

Philip

PHILIP was a friend of Andrew; he came from the town of Bethsaida where Peter and Andrew also came from. After Jesus asked him to follow him, Philip was so excited that he went to tell his friend Nathanael about Jesus of Nazareth and how he was the Promised One of God. Nathanael laughed, saying, "How could anyone important come from Nazareth?" Philip persuaded him to come and meet Jesus. When Nathanael actually met Jesus, he knew he was the Son of God.

Philip

Later on in Jesus' life, after he had ridden into Jerusalem on the donkey, some Greek people came up to Philip, who had a Greek name, to ask him if they could meet Jesus. Philip went and told his friend Andrew who introduced them to Jesus. Jesus knew that the time had come when people who were not Jewish would want to follow him.

What do you think?

1. Think about what Philip and Nathanael might have said to each other. Then act out the story.
2. What good news would you like to share with a friend?
3. How would being a fisherman have prepared Andrew for following Jesus? What qualities does a person whose job it is to catch fish possess?

Think further and investigate

1. Find out the day on which the feast of Saint Philip is celebrated. What are the Mass readings for that day? Why do you think they have been chosen?
2. What was so special about the Greeks asking to meet Jesus that Philip thought it was necessary to discuss it with Andrew?
3. Good friends give you support when you need it. How do you support your friends? What support do you expect from them?

Read what the Bible says

Read John 1:43–46 and John 12:20–23 in the order in which they are given here.

33

Matthew

TAX COLLECTORS are not very popular, as no one likes paying taxes. In Jesus' time the tax collectors worked for the Romans who had taken over Palestine. The collectors were often dishonest, charging people more than they should and keeping money for themselves. They were thought of as bad people.

It came as a surprise, then, when one day Jesus and his friends were passing by a tax collector's table and Jesus stopped, spoke to the collector, and invited him to follow him. The collector got up immediately and followed Jesus. His name was Matthew. He invited

Matthew

Jesus and his friends to come back to his house for a meal. When other people saw this, they criticized Jesus for eating and being friends with a sinner. Jesus explained that he had come especially to call sinners.

Matthew invited Jesus and his friends back to his house for a meal.

What do you think?

1. Why were the people surprised that Jesus asked Matthew to follow him?
2. What do you think Matthew might have done to make up for any dishonest actions he did as a tax collector?
3. Write a short prayer you could say to tell Jesus you are sorry for something you may have done wrong.

Think further and investigate

1. Look up the story of Jesus' encounter with another tax collector, Zaccheaus (Luke 19:1–10). What did he do to make up for his dishonesty? What did Jesus promise him in return? What can we learn from this story?
2. Look up the words used at the beginning of Mass in the penitential rite. Make up a saying of sorrow for your own sins, for example, "For the times we have .... Lord have mercy."

Read what the Bible says

Read Matthew 9:9–13.

Thomas

TWO SISTERS, Mary and Martha, sent for their friend Jesus when their brother, Lazarus, was very ill. They lived in Bethany, near Jerusalem. The Apostles knew that there were people who wanted to put Jesus to death, so it was dangerous. They tried to persuade him not to go. Jesus still insisted that he was going to Bethany. Then Thomas bravely spoke up and suggested that they should all go and be prepared to die with Jesus. However, the Apostles did not die with Jesus, but they were quite frightened after Jesus had been crucified, so for a short time they split up.

Thomas

When Jesus rose from the dead, he appeared to some of the Apostles. Thomas had not been there at the time and when the others told him that they had seen Jesus he did not believe them. In fact, Thomas said that he would need proof in order to believe. He would only believe if he could see and touch the marks of the nails in Jesus' hands and the wound in his side. A week later, Jesus appeared to the Apostles while Thomas was there. He looked at Thomas and invited

Jesus appears to the Apostles.

him to touch his wounds. Thomas had no doubts then; he called Jesus, "My Lord and God." Jesus explained to him that he was fortunate to be able to see him and believe, but that many people would believe in him who had not seen him.

What do you think?

1. What do you like about Thomas?
2. With some friends, act out the story of Thomas' meeting Jesus, using your own words.

Friends of Jesus

Thomas

Think further and investigate

1. Thomas said he was ready to die with Jesus. What does that show about him?
2. There are times when we find it hard to believe something that sensible people have told us. Why is that?
3. We have not seen God. What helps us to believe in him?
4. "Lord, I do believe, please help me in my doubts" is a well-known prayer. What do you think it means? Try to put this prayer into your own words.
5. Find a picture of Saint Thomas in a book, CD-ROM, or the Internet. Is it a good picture? What story does the picture show?

Read what the Bible says

Read John 11:1–16 and John 20:24–29 in the order in which they are given here.

Judas Iscariot

JUDAS was one of those chosen by Jesus to be his follower. He had a special job; he was in charge of looking after the money which belonged to Jesus and the Apostles.

In those days the roads were very dusty and people had to walk everywhere. They wore sandals, and so their feet became very dusty. Jesus and the Apostles were at the house of Lazarus and his sisters Martha and Mary. Mary covered Jesus' feet with perfumed oil and wiped them with her long hair. Judas got upset; he said he ➢

Friends of Jesus

Judas Iscariot

"I have sinned by betraying an innocent man to death!"... Judas threw the coins down in the Temple and left...

Matthew 27:4–5

thought the ointment ought to be sold to give money to the poor. The Gospel story tells us that Judas was not very honest and he was not thinking about the poor but about what he would do with the money himself.

Later on, Judas asked the chief priests if they would like him to show them where Jesus was so that they could arrest him. The chief priests were pleased with Judas' offer and promised to pay him thirty pieces of silver.

Judas shows the soldiers where Jesus is.

After the Last Supper, Jesus and the Apostles were praying in the garden of Gethsemane when Judas arrived with some soldiers. He showed them who Jesus was so they were able to arrest him. Later on, when Judas realized what the authorities were going to do with Jesus, he went back to the chief priests and threw the money they had given him onto the floor in front of them, saying how wrong he had been to betray Jesus. He went off very unhappy and sad inside.

What do you think?

1. What do you think about Judas? Can you think of some good as well as bad things about him?
2. Make up a short prayer to say you are sorry for the things you wish you had not done.

40

Judas Iscariot

Think further and investigate

1. Have you ever been let down by a friend? What did it feel like? Do you know why they acted that way? Were you able to be friends again?

2. Have you ever let down a friend yourself? Did you mean to do it? Why did you do it? How did you feel?

3. Write your own study of Judas and explain his character. Why did he act in some of the ways that he did?

4. Act out an imaginary conversation between Judas and Jesus after Jesus' Resurrection? What would they have said to each other?

5. Can you find a modern-day example of great forgiveness, maybe by someone who had been deeply hurt by violence or terrorism? What is special about the story?

Read what the Bible says

Read John 12:1–7, Matthew 26:14–16, Matthew 26:47–51, and Matthew 27:3–5 in the order in which they are given here.

Other Friends of Jesus

Jesus met many women and men as he traveled through the countryside. Some of his followers stayed at home and continued with their ordinary daily life, but supported Jesus by offering him hospitality and friendship. Luke in his Gospel (8:1–3) names some of the women who helped him: Mary of Magdala, Joanna, and Susanna. Some women followed Jesus throughout the time he was teaching and healing and were there when he died and witnessed his Resurrection (Matthew 27:55–56, Luke 23:55–56).

Mary of Magdala

MARY came from a small town on the coast of the Sea of Galilee called Magdala. Jesus had healed her of demons. We do not know exactly what the demons were; perhaps they were worries that Mary had, concerns which were weighing her down. After that meeting with Jesus, she became one of his faithful followers.

Mary never deserted Jesus; even when he was dying on the Cross she was there. After Jesus died, the Apostles buried his body quickly, because it was nearly the Sabbath day (Saturday); a time

Mary of Magdala

when Jewish people rest and do not work. Mary watched them do this and roll the heavy stone in front of the tomb. She took good care to remember where his tomb was, so she could return on Sunday after the Sabbath and anoint Jesus' body with oil so it was properly prepared for burial.

They found the stone rolled away from the entrance to the tomb, so they went in…

Luke 24:2–3

When Sunday morning arrived, Mary and some other women went to the tomb very early before it was even light. She was worried about how she would manage to move the heavy stone, but to her surprise when she got there it had been moved. The tomb was empty, she told Peter and John who were behind. They looked in the tomb and went home. Mary stayed near the tomb crying, because she did not understand what was happening. A man, who Mary thought was the gardener, spoke to her and asked her why she was crying. She told him. He said, "Mary," in a voice she immediately recognized. It was Jesus. Mary was very, very happy; she understood that Jesus had risen from the dead and was alive. She wanted to stay there with Jesus but he told her she had an important job to do for him, to go and tell the disciples that she had seen him and that he was going to return to God his Father. ➢

"Women why are you crying?"… Then she turned around and saw Jesus standing there…

John 20:13–14

She went running to Simon Peter…

John 20:2

What do you think?

1. Why do you think Mary followed Jesus?

2. Some of the Apostles did not believe Mary when she told them about Jesus' Resurrection. Have you ever had the experience of not being believed? What did it feel like? What can you do if no one believes you?

3. With some friends, act out the story of Mary meeting Jesus by the tomb. Use your own words.

Friends of Jesus

Mary of Magdala

Think further and investigate

1. Think how Mary felt on Saturday in the time after Jesus was buried and also when she went to the tomb on Sunday. Express those feelings as a poem or a drawing.

2. Mary was a witness of the Resurrection. Find out more about what it means to be a witness.

3. Use a weekday Missal to look up the feast of Saint Mary of Magdala (it may also be spelled Magdalene). What day is it celebrated? What do the readings and prayers of that day tell you?

4. Make up a prayer asking Mary of Magdala to pray for you. What special gift would you ask her to pray for you to receive?

Read what the Bible says

Read Luke 8:2, Matthew 27:55–66, Luke 23:55–56, John 20:1–2, and John 20:11–18 in the order in which they are given here.

Martha and Mary

MARTHA AND MARY lived with their brother, Lazarus, in the town of Bethany within easy walking distance of Jerusalem. They were special friends of Jesus; he often stayed with them when he visited Jerusalem. Although Martha and Mary were sisters, they had very different characters. Martha was a very good hostess and when Jesus came to stay she was busy rushing around cooking and seeing to everything, to make sure Jesus was comfortable and had what he needed. It was her way of telling Jesus how much she loved him. Mary on the other hand ➤

Friends of Jesus

Martha and Mary

was different; she liked to just sit by Jesus and talk to him and listen to his stories.

One day, when Jesus was at their house Martha got really upset with Mary for not helping her and asked Jesus to tell her so. Jesus told Martha not to worry so much about getting everything ready, but that the important thing in life was to listen to God's word. Jesus thought Mary had made a good choice by staying with him.

Martha was busy with all the work she had to do...

Based on Luke 10:40

 **What do you think?**

1. Brothers and sisters are often different in their attitudes; in what ways are you the same and what ways are you different from your brother or sister? (If you don't have a brother or sister, think of a friend.)
2. What is good about Martha's behavior?
3. What is good about Mary's behavior?
4. Make up a short prayer about always doing your best to be a good listener as well as a good helper.

Martha and Mary

Think further and investigate

1. Think of the conversation that may have taken place between Martha and Mary after Jesus had left the house after the visit told about on the preceding pages. Act or write out the story, trying to express each person's point of view.

2. Are you a Martha or a Mary type person or a bit of both? Think about your good points and make up a prayer to thank God for them.

3. In the time of Jesus, someone who sat listening at the feet of a teacher was someone who was training to be a rabbi. Why should this be an extraordinary thing for Mary to do?

Read what the Bible says

Read Luke 10:38–42, John 12:1–8, and Matthew 26:6–13 in the order in which they are given here.

Lazarus

LAZARUS lived in Bethany near Jerusalem, with his sisters Martha and Mary. They were all great friends of Jesus. He was very fond of them and often stayed with them.

Jesus was on the far side of the river Jordan when he received a message to say that Lazarus was very ill. Instead of going straight to Bethany, Jesus stayed where he was for two days longer. When Jesus and the Apostles eventually got near Bethany, Martha was there to meet him with the news that Jesus had arrived too late,

Lazarus

because Lazarus had died. Mary stayed in the house. There were lots of people there from Jerusalem who had come to sympathize with Martha and Mary.

...his heart was touched, and he was deeply moved.

John 11:33

Martha spoke to Jesus saying that she thought that if he had been there Lazarus would not have died, but even now she believed that he could help. Jesus told her that her brother Lazarus would rise again. Martha thought he meant at the end of the world. Jesus explained that he meant now. Martha went off to get Mary. When Mary saw Jesus, she cried and said she wished he had got there earlier and then Lazarus would not have died. Jesus was upset and he cried, too, because he loved Lazarus. Jesus asked where Lazarus had been buried. When they arrived at the tomb, Jesus asked for the stone sealing the entrance to be removed. Everyone wondered what he was going to do. Jesus prayed to his Father. Then in a loud voice he called out, "Lazarus, come out." Much to everyone's amazement Lazarus walked out of his tomb!

Everyone was filled with joy and was happy. Jesus had raised Lazarus from the dead. ➢

What do you think?

1. What would you do for your special friend?
2. Perhaps a person you loved died or maybe a family pet. How did you feel? What made you feel better?
3. Imagine that you are Lazarus. Tell someone what happened to you and how you felt about it.
4. We can pray for people who have died, asking God to give them happiness with him forever. Can you make up a prayer for those who have died?

Everyone was filled with joy to see Lazarus walk out of the tomb.

Friends of Jesus

Lazarus

Think further and investigate

1. What did you notice about the differing ways that Mary and Martha behaved?
2. The Apostles did not want Jesus to go to Bethany (see John 11:5-9). Why was it dangerous? (Clue: check the story of Thomas.)
3. What event in Jesus' life does this story remind you of?
4. Using a Missal look up and read some of the prayers that are used at a funeral. How do they reassure us?
5. Find Bethany on a map; the Gospel says it is two miles from Jerusalem. How long do you think this would take to walk there?
6. Look up John 12:9-11. Who was in danger and why?

Read what the Bible says

Read John 11:1-44.

Some People Who Helped Spread the Good News of Jesus

The next set of stories are about the people who helped spread the Good News of Jesus after he had returned to Heaven at the Ascension and after the Holy Spirit had come upon Mary and the Apostles. These friends of Jesus traveled around telling everyone about Jesus. They were missionaries. More and more people came to believe in Jesus, and churches were set up in many different places around the Mediterranean Sea. There are stories in the Acts of the Apostles in the New Testament which show how the Good News was spread and how Jesus' followers lived.

Paul

PAUL was originally called Saul. He was a Jew, but one born in a Roman city, so he was a Roman citizen. This was quite helpful to him at times because it meant he could only be judged by Roman law, not local law. Paul trained as a rabbi but he was also a tentmaker, since all rabbis had to have a means of earning their own living.

Paul never met Jesus when he was on earth. He was a member of the Jewish authority who wanted to get rid of the followers of Jesus. He was sent from Jerusalem to Damascus to round up the followers

Paul

of Jesus and bring them back to Jerusalem. As he was riding along, suddenly there was a bright light and Paul heard a voice saying to him, "Why are you persecuting me?" Paul asked who was speaking, "I am Jesus," the voice replied, "Go into the city and wait there, you will be told what to do."

So Ananias went, entered the house where Saul was, and placed his hands on him.

Acts 9:17

Paul went into Damascus. He could not see because the light had blinded him. For three days he stayed indoors praying and not eating or drinking. Meanwhile a man called Ananias, who was a follower of Jesus, received a message from God telling him to visit Paul. Ananias was a bit frightened, as he had heard how cruel Paul had been to Jesus' followers, but he did what God asked him.

Paul told Ananias what had happened. Ananias prayed with Paul and his sight was restored. Paul was baptized and became a disciple of Jesus.

Paul boarding a boat at the start of one of his missionary journeys.

Paul traveled to many different places telling people about Jesus. He spent a lot of his time with the Gentiles — that is, the people who were not Jews. He had many adventures on his travels; he was shipwrecked in the Mediterranean Sea and imprisoned several times. He wrote letters to the ➢

Friends of Jesus

Paul

...the ship hit a sandbank and went aground...

...the army officer wanted to save Paul... so he ordered all the men who could swim to jump overboard first and swim ashore...

Acts 27:41–43

people in the places he had visited. Sometimes he praised people for the good deeds they were doing and sometimes thanked them for money they sent him to help his missionary work. Sometimes he explained more of Jesus' message and occasionally he told people off for doing wrong. Many of these letters are in the New Testament. They are called epistles.

Eventually Paul was imprisoned in Rome and finally put to death by the Roman emperor Nero.

Paul wrote to many people while he was in prison.

What do you think?

1. What made Paul stop hating the followers of Jesus?
2. How do you think Ananias felt when he first met Paul?
3. If you traveled around like Paul what would you like to tell people about Jesus?

Paul

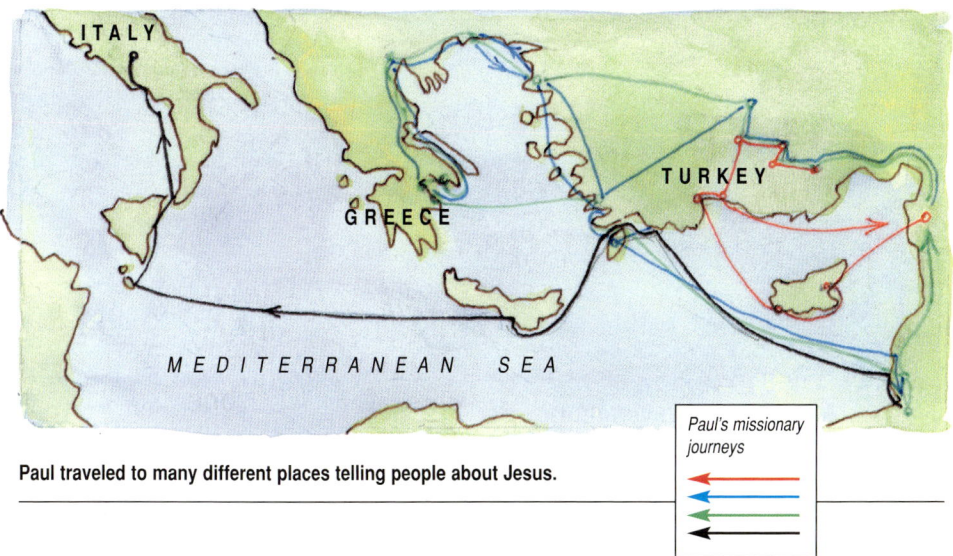

Paul traveled to many different places telling people about Jesus.

Paul's missionary journeys

Think further and investigate

1. Find a picture of Saint Paul from a book or CD-ROM or the Internet. What symbols are in the picture? What do you think these symbols mean and what do they tell you?

2. Look up the Letter to the Galatians, chapter 1, verses 6–9. What kind of letter is this? What is happening in Galatia? Read Galatians 6:1–5; what advice does Paul have to offer?

3. When is the feast of Saint Paul? With what other saint does he share this day? Why is Paul so important in the Church?

4. It takes courage to be a missionary. Choose a missionary you are interested in and read to discover something about that person's life.

Read what the Bible says

Read Acts 9:1–19.

Luke

LUKE came from Antioch, a town in Syria; he was a friend and companion of Paul. He was a doctor. He wrote one of the Gospels. He used some of Mark's Gospel to help him write it. Luke wrote his Gospel for those people who were not Jewish, the Gentiles. He shows how Jesus, although he came to bring the chosen Jewish people into the love of God, included other people as well. Here is a story that is in the Gospel of Luke.

Jesus was near a Samaritan village when he met ten men who had a dreadful skin disease called leprosy. They were not allowed to live in their village in case this disease spread to other people. As Jesus

Luke

approached, the lepers called out, "Jesus, master, have pity on us." Jesus healed them and told them to show themselves to the priest. That was so that they would be allowed back in the village. They all ran off except for one man, a Samaritan, who thanked Jesus for what he had done. Jesus was very pleased that he had remembered to thank God and praised him.

Luke wrote another book, also in the New Testament; it is called the Acts of the Apostles. It tells the story of how the Good News of Jesus spread after he had returned to Heaven. The Apostles lived together and shared what they had with each other. Every day they went to the Temple to pray and came home to break bread together the way Jesus had told them to do at the Last Supper.

What do you think?

1. Why is Luke an important person?
2. Luke was not one of Jesus' disciples so how did he know about the story of Jesus' life?
3. Why did Jesus praise the Samaritan leper?
4. Make up a thank-you prayer to Jesus for all he has given you.

Think further and investigate

1. What does the story from Luke's Gospel tell us about Jesus' attitude to people who are different from him? Remember Jesus was a Jew, and the leper was a Samaritan.
2. Luke describes how the early Christians lived in the Acts of the Apostles, especially in Acts 2:44–47. What do you think about this lifestyle? Make up a code of behavior for Christians today.
3. We do not usually use the expression, "breaking bread." Give some words that we do use today.

Read what the Bible says

Read Luke 17:11–19.

Barnabas

BARNABAS was a Jewish man who came from the island of Cyprus. His name was Joseph but the Apostles called him "Barnabas," which means *someone who encourages others*. Barnabas joined the group of Jesus' followers who were spreading the Good News of Jesus at the very beginning of the Church. Barnabas owned a field; he knew that Jesus' followers shared everything, so he sold his field. He gave the money to the Apostles so they could help those people who were poor.

Barnabas

The Church was spreading and the people of Antioch in Syria became followers of Jesus. When the Apostles in Jerusalem heard about this they decided to send Barnabas there to encourage the Greek people, because he was a good man who was faithful to Jesus' message of love. Barnabas was so pleased with the Church in Antioch that he went off to Tarsus to look for Paul to tell him. When he found him he brought Paul to Antioch. Paul and Barnabas stayed there for a year teaching people about Jesus' message. It was there that the followers were first called "Christians."

After a year, Paul and Barnabas set off together to travel to other countries and towns to bring people the Good News. Like Paul, Barnabas helped people who were not Jewish to belong to the Church.

What do you think?

1. Do you think that Barnabas' nickname of encourager was a good one for him? What makes you think that?
2. Do you like being encouraged? How does it help you? Give an example of when someone encouraged you.
3. Barnabas shared what he had by selling his field and giving away the money. What does it feel like to share?
4. Look at the word "Christian." How many words can you get out of it by using the letters? What does it tell you about the meaning of the word?
5. Barnabas was a good man. How can we tell a good person? What are they like?

Paul and Barnabas teaching in Antioch.

Friends of Jesus ───────────────

Barnabas

Think further and investigate

1. Find a map of Paul's journey from a Bible, encyclopedia, or through the use of the Internet. Find also Jerusalem and the island of Cyprus. Imagine how Paul and Barnabas traveled around in those days.
2. We use the word "Christian" quite often today. How would you describe a Christian?
3. If you were Barnabas, what would you want to tell the people of Antioch?

Read what the Bible says

Read Acts 4:36–37 and Acts 11:20–26.

Notes for Parents and Teachers

The scope of the stories in the *Friends of Jesus*

This is a book about the people Jesus met during his life on earth, his family, and his friends. There are also stories about people who helped spread the Good News of Jesus after he had returned to heaven. Some of the stories will provide a way into understanding important events in the life of Jesus, such as his birth, baptism, Transfiguration, death, and Resurrection. Every story has suggested activities suitable for a range of ages and interests.

The purpose of this book

It is hoped that this book will provide children with a scripturally accurate picture of some of the people they will find in the New Testament. From these stories, it is hoped that they will make a link to the liturgical calendar of the Church and that these people will have something to say to the children in their own lives. Many of the stories are from more than one book of the New Testament.

Scriptural accuracy

No apocryphal writings have been included; for instance, there is no mention of Mary's parents, as the Scriptures do not tell us anything about them. Joseph is described as being a carpenter, which is about the nearest translation of the Greek "tekton," which refers to building with hard materials. There is some use of the traditional understanding of the Gospels; for example, in the story of John, it is accepted that the beloved disciple is in fact John; scholars today might question that acceptance.

John's Gospel (19:28) speaks of Mary's sister being with Mary at the foot of the cross. The New Testament speaks in a number of places of Jesus' brothers as his family. The words "brother" or "sister" as used in the Bible may mean relative in its widest sense, so it is not possible to give it the meaning we have today. Tradition and doctrine has it that Mary did not have any other children. In this book the word "apostle" is used for the twelve chosen followers of Jesus, but it would also be correct to call them disciples.

How to use this book

Parents and children could read these stories together at home or children could read them on their own and use them for research and investigation. In school they could provide a useful follow-up to many areas of study. There are ideas for ways of thinking creatively and meditatively about the life of the person in the story. For young children, there are some simple activities; and the illustrations will help them remember and enjoy the stories. ➢

Friends of Jesus

For older children, the section Think Further and Investigate provides some Scripture references to follow up and ideas for further research. There is often a link to the liturgical calendar of the Church.

Pronouncing Glossary

Ananias (an-uh-**nigh**-us): *a disciple sent by God to bring Paul into the Christian community*
Antioch (**an**-tee-ok): *a town in what is now Syria*
Barnabas (**bar**-nuh-bus): *companion of Paul on his first missionary journey*
Bethsaida (beth-**say**-duh): *place on the shore of the Sea of Galilee*
Boanaerges (**bo**-uh-nur-jez): *Jesus' nickname for John and Peter*
Capernaum (kah-**pur**-nee-uhm): *ancient place on the Sea of Galilee*
Cyprus (**sigh**-pruhs): *island in the Mediterranean Sea near Turkey*
Damascus (duh-**mass**-kuhs): *ancient city in what is now Syria*
Galilee (**gal**-uh-lee): *a region in Israel, often site of Jesus' ministry*
Gethsemane (geth-**sem**-uh-nee): *garden near Jerusalem where Jesus prayed before his death*
high priest (high **preest**): *head of the priests at the Temple in Jerusalem*
Jairus (**jair**-uhs): *Jewish official who asked Jesus to heal his daughter*
Jerusalem (juh-**roo**-suh-lem): *city in the land of Israel where Jesus came on pilgrimages and where he was crucified, died, buried, and rose from the dead.*
Judas Iscariot (**joo**-duhs is-**car**-ee-ot): *apostle who gave Jesus over to his executioners*
Last Supper (last **sup**-per): *final meal Jesus ate with his disciples before his death*
Lazarus (**laz**-er-uhs): *brother of Mary and Martha whom Jesus raised from the dead*
Magdala (**mahg**-dah-lah): *a place near the Sea of Galilee, thought to be Mary Magdalene's hometown*
Magnificat (mahg-**nehf**-ee-caht): *song of praise sung by Mary on her visit to Elizabeth*
Messiah (me-**sigh**-ah): *title used for Jesus*
Nazareth (**naz**-er-uth): *small village in Galilee where Jesus lived as a youth*
Pentecost (pen-tuh-cost): *day when the Holy Spirit descended on the apostles*
Samaritan (suh-**mare**-ih-tahn): *a person from the district of Samaria*
Simeon (**sim**-eeh-uhn): *old man who recognized Jesus as the Messiah at his Presentation in the Temple*
synagogue (**sin**-uh-gohg): *places of prayer where a Jewish community gathers*
Temple (**tem**-puhl): *sacred worship place for Jews in Jerusalem*
Zaccheaus (zah-**kee**-uhs): *wealthy tax collector who became Jesus' host and disciple*
Zebedee (**zeb**-eh-dee): *father of the apostles James and John*
Zechariah (zek-eh-**righ**-uh): *husband of Elizabeth, Mary's cousin*